FUN FACTS ABOUT
SALAMANDERS!

Carmen Bredeson

Enslow Elementary
an imprint of
Enslow Publishers, Inc.
40 Industrial Road
Box 398
Berkeley Heights, NJ 07922
USA
http://www.enslow.com

CONTENTS

WORDS TO KNOW

gills (GIHLZ)—Parts used for breathing underwater.

moist (MOYST)—A little wet.

newt (NOOT)—A kind of salamander.

pore (POR)—A tiny hole in an animal's skin.

venom (VEH nuhm)—A liquid from an animal that causes sickness or death.

PARTS OF A SALAMANDER

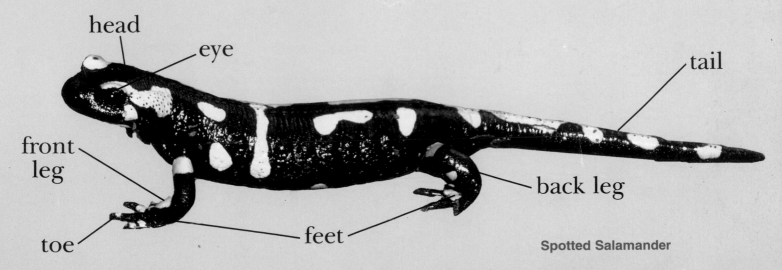

head

eye

tail

front leg

back leg

toe

feet

Spotted Salamander

3

WHAT DO SALAMANDERS LOOK LIKE?

Red Salamander

Salamanders have long bodies and tails. They have smooth, **moist** skin. Some people think they look like lizards, but salamanders are not lizards. They are close cousins of frogs and toads.

5

WHERE DO SALAMANDERS LIVE?

Salamanders are quiet, shy animals. They like damp, cool places. Some salamanders live on land. They hide under rocks and tree trunks. Salamanders that live in water hide in weeds and mud.

Spring Salamander

Eastern Tiger Salamander

Chinese Giant Salamander

HOW BIG ARE SALAMANDERS?

Most salamanders are less than ten inches long. But giant salamanders can grow to be five feet long. Pigmy (PIG mee) salamanders are tiny. They can be as small as your little finger.

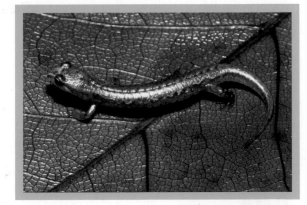

Pigmy Salamander

9

WHAT DO SALAMANDERS EAT?

Salamanders eat many kinds of insects, spiders, snails, and worms. Some salamanders even eat other salamanders!

A salamander watches a worm crawl by. The salamander's tongue shoots out of its mouth. ZAP! GULP! It swallows the worm whole.

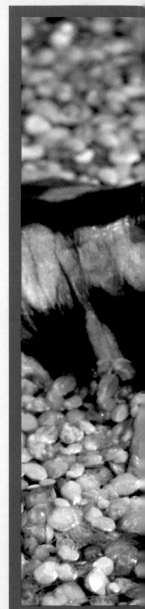

Salamanders do not have teeth for chewing.

Tiger Salamander

This frog is eating
a Marbled Newt.

WHAT EATS SALAMANDERS?

Snakes, birds, frogs, and other small animals eat salamanders. Salamanders stay hidden all day. They come out at night to hunt for food. It is harder to see salamanders at night. This is one way they stay safe.

HOW DO SALAMANDERS STAY SAFE FROM THEIR ENEMIES?

Mud Salamander

Many salamanders have slime on their skin. The slime can taste bad or have **venom** in it. Bright colors on the skin warn animals that the salamander may not be safe to eat.

14

Barred Tiger Salamander

Axolotl Salamander

gills

16

HOW DO SALAMANDERS BREATHE?

All salamanders breathe air through their skin. The skin has millions of tiny holes called **pores**. Air comes in through these pores. Some salamanders also have lungs or **gills** to help them breathe.

HOW DO SALAMANDERS GET AROUND?

Most salamanders have four legs. The legs are so short that the salamander's belly rubs along the ground. Salamanders that live in water do not need to walk. They swim like fish and have only two tiny legs.

The Rio Grande Lesser Siren has only two legs.

Northwestern Salamander

WHAT IS THE
LIFE CYCLE
OF A
SALAMANDER?

1. The mother salamander lays eggs in the water. The eggs are covered with clear jelly.

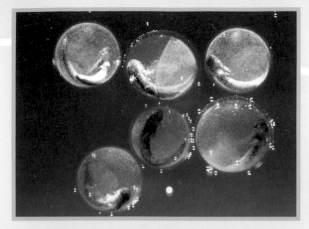

2. Through the clear jelly, watch the little salamanders grow.

3. After a few weeks, the babies hatch and swim away.

4. This Spotted Salamander is all grown up.

LEARN MORE

BOOKS

Clarke, Barry. *Amphibian*. New York: Dorling Kindersley
Publishing, 2005.

Murray, Julie. *Salamanders*. Edna, Minn: ABDO Publishing
Company, 2005.

Sill, Cathryn. *About Amphibians*. Atlanta, Ga.:
Peachtree Publishers, 2004.

Red-Spotted Newt

WEB SITES

Enchanted Learning

<http://www.enchantedlearning.com/subjects/amphibians/
Salamanderprintout.shtml>

San Diego Zoo

<http://www.sandiegozoo.org/animalbytes/
t-salamander.html>

Smithsonian National Zoo

<http://www.nationalzoo.si.edu/
Animals/ReptilesAmphibians/
ForKids>

Spotted Salamander

INDEX

Tiger Salamander

A Note About Reptiles and Amphibians:

Amphibians can live on land or in water. Frogs, toads, and salamanders are amphibians.
Reptiles have skin covered with scales. Snakes, alligators, turtles, and lizards are reptiles.

Enslow Elementary, an imprint of Enslow Publishers, Inc.
Enslow Elementary® is a registered trademark of Enslow Publishers, Inc.

Copyright © 2008 by Carmen Bredeson

All rights reserved.

No part of this book may be reproduced by any means
without the written permission of the publisher.

Library of Congress Cataloging-in-Publication Data

Bredeson, Carmen.
    Fun facts about salamanders! / Carmen Bredeson.
        p. cm. — (I like reptiles and amphibians!)
    Includes bibliographical references and index.
    ISBN-13: 978-0-7660-2790-9
    ISBN-10: 0-7660-2790-2
    1. Salamanders—Juvenile literature. I. Title. II. Series.
QL668.C2B69 2006
597.8'5—dc22   2006015916

Printed in the United States of America

10 9 8 7 6 5 4 3 2 1

Every effort has been made to locate all copyright holders of material used in this
book. If any errors or omissions have occurred, corrections will be made in future
editions of this book.

To Our Readers: We have done our best to make sure all Internet Addresses in this
book were active and appropriate when we went to press. However, the author and the
publisher have no control over and assume no liability for the material available on
those Internet sites or on other Web sites they may link to. Any comments or
suggestions can be sent by e-mail to comments@enslow.com or to the address on the
back cover.

Photo Credits: © age fotostock / Superstock, p. 12; © Barry Mansell / naturepl.com,
p. 18; © David M. Dennis/Animals Animals, p. 15; © G. & C. Merker / Visuals
Unlimited, p. 23; © Gerold and Cynthia Merker/Visuals Unlimited, p. 19; © Gilbert
Twiest / Visuals Unlimited, p. 20; © Jim Merli / Visuals Unlimited, p. 7; © Joe
McDonald / Visuals Unlimited, p. 6; © 2006 JupiterImages, Corp. / Marty Cordano,
p. 11; © NHPA / Joe Blossom, p. 13; PhotoResearchers, Inc., p. 14; © Robert Lubeck/
Animals Animals, p. 21 (3); Shutterstock, pp. 1, 3, 22; © Stephen Dalton / Animals
Animals, pp. 16–17; Suzanne Collins, p. 9; Suzanne L. & Joseph T. Collins/Photo
Researchers, Inc., pp. 4–5; © Ted Levin / Animals Animals, p. 21 (2); Tom McHugh/
Photo Researchers, Inc., p. 8; © Zigmund Leszczynski / Animals Animals, p. 21 (4).

Cover Photograph: © Gerold and Cynthia Merker / Visuals Unlimited

Series Science Consultant:
Raoul Bain
Herpetology Biodiversity Specialist
Center for Biodiversity and
    Conservation
American Museum of Natural History
New York, NY

Series Literacy Consultant:
Allan A. De Fina, Ph.D.
Past President of the New Jersey
    Reading Association
Professor, Department of Literacy Education
New Jersey City University
Jersey City, NJ